the Dobermann

A guide to selection, care, nutrition, upbringing, training, health, breeding sports and play

Contents

Foreword

The book you are holding is a basic 'owners manual' for everyone owning a Dobermann and also for those who are considering buying a Dobermann. What we have done in this book is to give the information to help the (future) owner of a Dobermann look after his or her pet responsibly. Too many people still buy a pet before really understanding what they're about to get into.

This book goes into the broad history of the Dobermann, the breed standard and some pros and cons of buying a Dobermann. You will also find essential information on feeding, initial training and an introduction in reproduction. Finally we give attention to (day-to-day) care, health and some breed-specific ailments.

Based on this information, you can buy a Dobermann, having thought it through carefully, and keep it as a pet in a responsible manner. Our advice, though, is not just to leave it to this small book. A correctly brought-up and well-trained dog is more than just a dog. Invest a little extra in a puppy training course or an obedience course. There are also excellent books available that go deeper into certain aspects than is possible here.

About Pets

A Publication of About Pets.

co-publisher United Kingdom
Kingdom Books
PO9 5TL, England

ISBN 1852791896
First printed
September 2003

Original title: *de Dobermann*

Photos:
Rob Doolaard, Rob Dekker, J. de Kruyk,
B. van der Vliet, A. Griekspoor
and Katja Brom-ter Beek

Printed in Italy

In general

The Dobermann or, more correctly, the Dobermann Pinscher, is a muscular, medium-sized, powerfully built dog with a proud posture that has many enthusiasts across the world.

It's not always the easiest dog for strangers to deal with, but its master and family mean everything to a Dobermann. This characteristic makes it not only a good pet and companion, but also an excellent working dog. Its high level of intelligence helps it in any sport and ensures that life with a Dobermann is never boring.

Origins

The Dobermann is a relatively young breed and doesn't have centuries of history behind it like some other breeds. But despite that, its history is interesting. In 1834, the spiritual father of the breed, Friedrich Louis Dobermann was born in the small German town of Apolda. According to legend, he was a tax collector, skinner and the town's official dog-catcher, with the legal right to catch any stray dogs.
He bred especially aggressive dogs from this stock. The key role in the development of the Dobermann was played by the so-called "butchers' dogs", which under the conditions at that time counted as a relatively pure breed. They were more or less the ancestors of today's Rottweiler mixed with a type of black sheepdog with rust-red markings found in Thüringen. Friedrich Dobermann bred with these dogs during the 1870's, and he eventually produced the dog he was looking for: a working dog that was not only alert, but was also a companionable dog for house and home. They were then also often used as guard dogs and police dogs. This quickly led to the nick-

name "Gendarme Dog". At the beginning of the twentieth century, the Dobermann was officially recognised as a police dog. As far as hunting was concerned, the Dobermann was mainly used to fight predatory game.

Breed standard

A standard has been developed for all breeds recognised by the Kennel Club for the UK (and in Europe by the F.C.I. - the umbrella organisation for Western European kennel clubs). Officially approved kennel clubs in the member countries provide a translation. This standard provides a guideline for breeders and judges. It is something of an ideal that dogs of the breed must strive to match. With some breeds, dogs are already bred that match the ideal. Other breeds have a long way to go. There is a list of defects for each breed. These can be serious defects that disqualify the dog, and it will be excluded from breeding. Permitted defects are not serious, but do cost points in a show.

The UK Kennel Club breed standard for the Dobermann

General appereance:
Medium size, muscular and elegant with well set body. Of proud carriage, compact and tough. Capable of great speed.

Characteristics:
Intelligent and firm of character, loyal and obedient.

Temperament:
Bold and alert. Shyness or viciousness very highly undesirable.

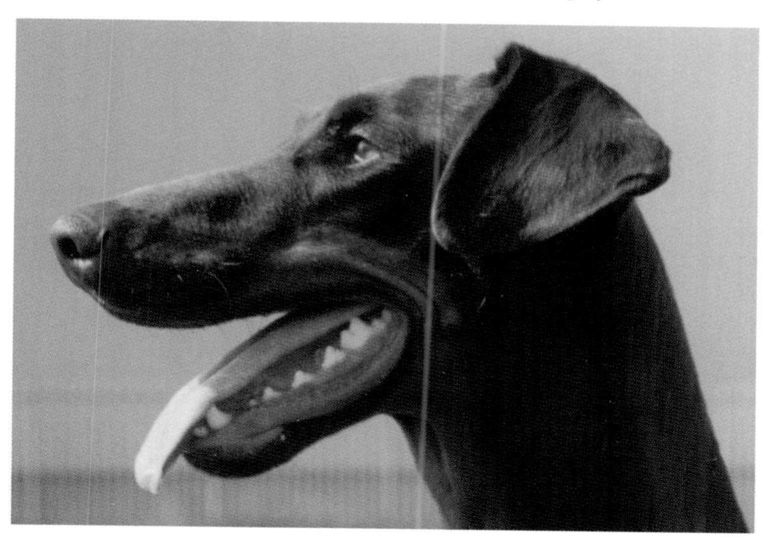

Head & Skull:
In proportion to body. Long, well filled out under eyes and clean cut, with good depth of muzzle. Seen from above and side, resembles an elongated blunt wedge. Upper part of head flat and free from wrinkle. Top of skull flat slight stop; muzzle line extending parallel to top line of skull. Cheeks flat, lips tight. Nose solid black in black dogs, solid dark brown in brown dogs, solid dark grey in blue dogs and light brown in fawn dogs. Head out of balance in proportion to body, dish faced, snipy or cheeky very highly undesirable.

Eyes:
Almond-shaped, not round, moderately deep set, not prominent, with lively, alert expression. Iris of uniform colour, ranging from

medium to darkest brown in black dogs, the darker shade being more desirable. In browns, blues or fawns, colour of iris blends with that of markings, but not of lighter hue than markings; light eyes in black dogs highly undesirable.

Ears:
Small, neat, set high on head. Normally dropped, but may be erect.

Mouth:
Well developed, solid and strong with a complete dentition and a perfect, regular and complete scissor bite, i.e. the upper teeth closely overlapping the lower teeth and set square to the jaws. Evenly placed teeth. Undershot, overshot or badly arranged teeth highly undesirable.

Neck:
Fairly long and lean, carried with considerable nobility, slightly convex and in proportion to shape of dog. Region of nape very muscular. Dewlap and loose skin undesirable.

Forequarters:
Shoulder blade and upper arm meet at an angle of 90 degrees. Shoulder blade and upper arm approximately equal in length. Short upper arm relative to shoulder blade highly undesirable. Legs seen from front and side, perfectly straight and parallel to each other from elbow to pastern; muscled and sinewy, with round bone in proportion to body structure. Standing or gaiting, elbows lies close to brisket.

Body:
Square, height measured vertically from ground to highest point at withers equal to length from forechest to rear projection of upper thigh. Forechest well developed. Back short and firm, straight topline sloping slightly from withers to croup; bitches may be slightly longer to loin. Ribs deep and well sprung, reaching to elbow. Belly fairly well tucked up. Long, weak, or roach backs highly undesirable.

Hindquarters:
Legs parallel to each other and moderately wide apart. Pelvis falling away from spinal column at an angle of about 30 degrees. Croup well filled out. Hindquarters well developed and muscular, long, well bent stifle; hocks turning neither in nor out. When standing, hock to heel perpendicular to the ground.

Feet:
Well arched, compact, and catlike, turning neither in nor out. All dewclaws removed. Long, flat deviating feel and/or weak pasterns highly undesirable.

Tail:
Customarily docked at first or second joint; appears to be a

continuation of spine without material drop.

Gait:
Elastic, free, balanced and vigorous, with good reach in forequarters and driving power in hindquarters. When trotting, should have strong rear drive, with apparent rotary motion of hindquarters. Rear and front legs thrown neither in nor out. Back remains strong and firm.

Coat:
Smooth, short, hard, thick and close lying. Imperceptible undercoat on neck permissible. Hair forming a ridge on back of neck and/or along spine highly undesirable.

Colour:
Definite black, brown, blue or fawn (Isabella) only, with rust red markings. Markings to be sharply defined, appearing above each eye, on muzzle, throat and forechest, on all legs and feet and below tail. White markings on any kind highly undesirable.

Size:
Ideal height at withers: Dog 69 cms (27 ins); Bitches 65 cms (25 1/2ins). Considerable deviation from this ideal undesirable.

Faults:
Any departure from the foregoing points should be considered a fault and the seriousness with which the fault should be regarded should be in exact proportion to its degree.

Note:
Male animals should have two apparently normal testicles fully descended into the scrotum.

Note:
A dog may be disqualified by the General Committee of The kennel Club from any award whether an objection has been lodged or not, if proven, among other things to have been (I) totally blind (ii) deaf, (iii) prevented from breeding as a result of a surgical operation except that this shall not apply to an animal that has progeny registered at The Kennel Club and except as provided in Regulations for the Preparation of Dogs for Exhibition –F (Annex B).

Breed standard by courtesy of the Kennel Club of Great Britain.

Buying a Dobermann

Once you've made that properly considered decision to buy a dog, there are several options. Should it be a puppy, an adult dog, or even an older dog? Should it be a bitch or dog, a pedigree dog or a cross?

Of course, the question also comes up as to where to buy your dog - from a private person, a reliable breeder or an animal shelter? For you and the animal, it's vital to get these questions sorted out in advance. You want a dog that will fit your circumstances properly. With a puppy, you get a playful energetic housemate that will easily adapt to a new environment. If you want something quieter, an older dog is a good choice.

Pros and cons of the Dobermann

As you've already read, the Dobermann is a nice companion, strongly focussed on its master. If it gets enough exercise, it will be very calm at home. Its body is built for action and a walk around the block three times a day is definitely not enough. Besides being let out regularly, a Dobermann needs a good run for at least one hour per day. Anything more is very welcome. Build a puppy up to this very gradually. Its bones still consist partly of soft cartilage and can quickly become deformed if overloaded. Even if you'd love to be out with your puppy all day, remember that you have its whole lifetime ahead of you to go for stiff walks with it. Try to provide for variety during your walks. Hide a ball and get your dog to search for it, or jog together. This variety will keep your Dobermann's mind active (something that is often forgotten).

Many people think of Dobermanns only as frightening guard dogs behind a fence. Sadly, some people consciously choose the breed because of that image, without thinking of other aspects. Choosing for the Dobermann (or any other breed) that way is disastrous. Of course, the Dobermann was originally bred as a watchdog, but it is far more than just that! It is a courageous and persevering dog that is used to taking matters into its own hands and, if it has to, taking care of its own well-being.

These characteristics make the Dobermann unique, but also mean that it's not a dog that will suit everybody. A Dobermann needs a lot of exercise and can be very dominant. It can also be a nuisance at times because, with its intelligence, it can happily solve "problems" on its own. The Dobermann therefore needs a strong, rigorous master who can give it what its history demands.

Male or female?

Whether you choose a male or a female puppy, or an adult dog or bitch, is an entirely personal decision. A male typically needs more leadership because he tends to be more dominant by nature. He will try to play boss over other dogs and, if he gets the chance, over people too. In the wild, the most dominant dog (or wolf) is always the leader of the pack. In many cases this is a male. A bitch is much more focussed on her master, she sees him as the pack leader.

A puppy test is good for defining the kind of character a young dog will develop. During a test one usually sees that a dog is more

dominant than a bitch. You can often quickly recognise the bossy, the adventurous and the cautious characters. So visit the litter a couple of times early on. Try to pick a puppy that suits your own personality. A dominant dog, for instance, needs a strong hand. It will often try to see how far it can go. You must regularly make it clear who's the boss, and that it must obey all the members of the family.

When bitches are sexually mature, they will go into season. On average, a bitch is in season twice a year for about two or three weeks. This is the fertile period when she can become pregnant. Particularly in the second half of her season, she will want to go looking for a dog to mate with. A male dog will show more masculine traits once he is sexually mature. He will make sure other dogs know what territory is his by urinating as often as possible in as many places as he can. He is also difficult to restrain if there's a bitch in season nearby. As far as normal care is concerned there is little difference between a dog and a bitch.

Puppy or adult?

After you've made the decision for a male or female, the next question comes up. Should it be a puppy or an adult dog? Your household circumstances usually play a major role here.

Of course, it's great having a sweet little puppy in the house, but bringing up a young dog requires a lot of time. In the first

year of its life it learns more than during the rest of its life. This is the period when the foundations are laid for elementary matters such as house-training, obedience and social behaviour. You must reckon with the fact that your puppy will keep you busy for a couple of hours a day, certainly in the first few months. You won't need so much time with a grown dog. It has already been brought up, but this doesn't mean it won't need correcting from time to time.

A puppy will no doubt leave a trail of destruction in its wake for the first few months. With a little bad luck, this will cost you a number of rolls of wallpaper, some good shoes and a few socks. In the worst case you'll be left with some chewed furniture. Some puppies even manage to tear curtains from their rails. With good upbringing this 'vandalism' will quickly disappear, but you won't have to worry about this if you get an older dog.

The greatest advantage of a puppy, of course, is that you can bring it up your own way. And the upbringing a dog gets (or doesn't get) is a major influence on its whole character. Finally, financial aspects may play a role in your choice. A puppy is generally (much) more expensive than an adult dog, not only in purchase price but also in 'maintenance'. A puppy needs to go to the vet's more often for the necessary vaccinations and check-ups. Overall, bringing up a puppy involves a good deal of energy, time and money, but you have its upbringing in your own hands. An adult dog costs less money and time, but its character is already formed. You should also try to find out about the background of an adult dog. Its previous owner may have formed its character in somewhat less positive ways.

Ten golden puppy rules

1 Walk your puppy in doses followed by one hour play, a feed and then three hours sleep.
2 Don't let your puppy run endlessly after a ball or stick.
3 Don't let your puppy romp wildly with large, heavy dogs.
4 Never let your puppy play on a full tummy.
5 Don't give your puppy anything to drink straight after a meal.
6 Don't let your puppy walk up and down steps for the first year. Be careful with shiny floors.
7 Don't add supplements to ready-made food.
8 Watch out for your puppy's weight. Being overweight can lead to bone abnormalities.
9 Give your puppy a quiet place to sleep.
10 Pick your puppy up carefully, one hand under its chest, the other under its hindquarters.

Two dogs?

Having two or more dogs in the house is not just nice for us, but also for the animals themselves. Dogs get a lot of pleasure from their own company. After all, they are pack animals.

If you're sure that you want two young dogs, it's best not to buy them at the same time. Bringing a dog up and establishing the bond between dog and master takes time, and you need to give a lot of attention to your dog in this phase. Having two puppies in the house means you have to divide your attention between them. Apart from that, there's a danger that they will focus on one another rather than on their master. Buy the second pup when the first is (almost) an adult.

Two adult dogs can happily be brought into the home together, as long as they're used to each other. If this is not the case, then they have to go through that process. This is usually best achieved by letting them get to know each other on neutral territory. This prevents fights for territory. On neutral territory, perhaps an acquaintance's garden where neither dog has been before, both dogs are basically equal. Once they've got to know each other, you can take them both home, and they can sort out the hierarchy there amongst themselves. In any event, don't get involved in trying to 'arbitrate'. That is human, but for the dog that's at the top of the pecking order it's like having its position undone. It will only make the dog more dominant in behaviour, with all the consequences. Once the hierarchy is established, most dogs can get along fine together.

Getting a puppy when the first dog is somewhat older often has a positive effect on the older dog. The influence of the puppy almost seems to give it a second childhood. The older dog, if it's been well brought up, can help with the up-bringing of the puppy. Young dogs like to imitate the behaviour of their elders. Don't forget to give both dogs the same amount of attention. Take both out alone at least once per day during the first eighteen months. Give the older dog enough opportunity to get some peace and quiet. It won't want an enthusiastic youngster running around under its feet all the time. Moreover, a puppy needs plenty of sleep and may have to have the brakes put on it once in a while.

The combination of a male and female needs special attention and it's good advice to get a second dog of the same sex. This will avoid a lot of problems. Sterilisation and castration is, of course, one solution, but it's a final one. A sterilised or castrated animal can never reproduce.

A dog and children

Dogs and children are a great combination. They can play together and get great pleasure out of each other's company. Moreover, children need to learn how to handle living beings; they develop respect and a sense of responsibility by caring for a dog (or other pets). However sweet a dog is, children must understand that it is an animal and not a toy. A dog isn't comfortable when it's being messed around with. It can become frightened, timid and even aggressive. So make it clear what a dog likes and what it doesn't.

Look for ways the child can play with the dog, perhaps a game of hide and seek where the child hides and the dog has to find it. Even a simple tennis ball can give enormous
pleasure. Children must learn to leave a dog in peace when it doesn't want to play any more. The dog must also have its own place where it's not disturbed. Have children help with your dog's care as much as possible. A strong bond will be the result.

The arrival of a baby also means changes in the life of a dog.

Before the birth you can help get the dog acquainted with the new situation. Let it sniff at the new things in the house and it will quickly accept them. When the baby has arrived involve the dog as much as possible in day-by-day events, but make sure it gets plenty of attention too. NEVER leave a dog alone with young children. Crawling infants sometimes make unexpected movements, which can easily frighten a dog. And infants are hugely curious, and may try to find out whether the tail is really fastened to the dog, or whether its eyes come out, just like they do with their cuddly toys. But a dog is a dog and it will defend itself when it feels threatened.

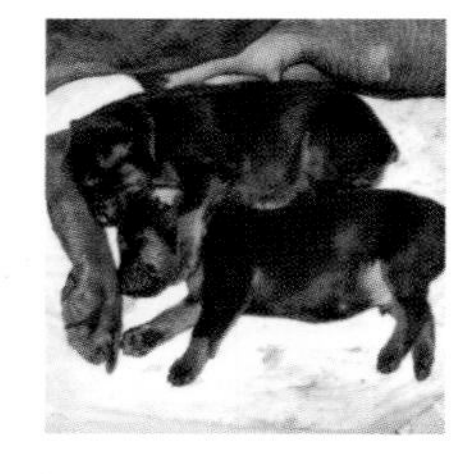

Where to buy

There are various ways of acquiring a dog. The decision for a puppy or an adult dog will also define for the most part where to buy your dog.

If it's to be a puppy, then you need to find a breeder with a litter. If you chose a popular breed, like the Dobermann, there is choice enough. But you may also face the problem that there are so many puppies on sale that have only been bred for profit's sake. You can see how many puppies are for sale by looking in the regional newspaper every Saturday. Some of these dogs have a pedigree, but many don't. These breeders often don't watch out for breed-specific illnesses and any hereditary breding faults and defects; puppies are separated from their mother as fast as possible and are thus insufficiently socialised. Never buy a puppy that is too young, or whose mother you weren't able to see.

Fortunately there are also enough bona-fide breeders of Dobermanns. Try to visit a number of breeders before you actually buy your puppy. Check the parent dogs' paper to ensure they were free of hip dysplasia (HD). Ask if the breeder is prepared to help you after you've bought your puppy, and to help you find solutions for any problems that may come up.

If you're looking for an adult dog, it's best to contact the breed association, who often help place adult dogs that can no longer be kept by their owners because of personal circumstances (impulse buying, moving home, divorce etc.).

Things to watch out for

Buying a puppy is no simple matter. You must pay attention to the following:

- Never buy a puppy on impulse, even if it is love at first sight. A dog is a living being that will need care and attention over a long period. It is not a toy that you can put away when you're finished with it.

- Take a good look at the mother. Is she calm, nervous, aggressive, well cared-for or neglected? The behaviour and condition of the mother is not only a sign of the quality of the breeder, but also of the puppy you're about to buy.
- Avoid buying a puppy whose mother has been kept only in a kennel. A young dog needs as many different impressions as possible in its first few months, including living in a family group. It gets used to people and possibly other pets. Kennel dogs miss these experiences and are inadequately socialised.
- Always ask to see the parents' papers (vaccination certificates, pedigrees, official reports on health examinations, inspection reports, certificates).

- Never buy a puppy younger than eight weeks.
- Put all agreements with the breeder in writing. A model agreement is available from the breed association.

The first few days

The first days in its new home are an enormous change for your puppy. It needs all the attention and love it deserves. If you can, arrange to pick up your puppy as early as possible on a Saturday morning. Then you've got all weekend to give it your attention and to help your puppy get used to its new surroundings.

Once at home, carry your puppy inside in the right way. Slide one hand under its bottom and use your other hand to wrap protectively around it. Before you go indoors, see whether it wants to do its business at a spot you've picked. If it does, reward it immediately and effusively.

Once in the house, try to let your puppy get as much rest as possible. It must have the opportunity to get used to everything. Place a bowl of water (food comes later) at its new, fixed place. Bring your puppy to its water bowl and let it take a drink. If it doesn't want to, don't try to force it. You have to keep remembering that, for your puppy, everything is totally strange, and it first wants to check everything out and be sure everything is as it should be.

Also introduce your puppy to its sleeping place. This must be dry and draught-free. Choose a place in the house where it's not laying in people's way, but where it can see everybody. The latter is most important, because your puppy will want to be sure that its pack is all together, and that it's part of that pack. Leave all doors open, except for those that it should never go through in the future. Give it all the time it needs to explore its surroundings in peace, so don't call it! .

After some time, your puppy will certainly be tired. If you remain still, at some moment it will fall asleep somewhere in the room. This will certainly not be the place you picked as its bed, but that will take care of itself eventually.

For the time being, stick to the feeding times the breeder has given you. An eight-week old puppy must certainly be fed four times a day. If you stick to the rule that it should go its own way as much as possible the first few days, your puppy will quickly get used to its new environment.

Perils of the night

Ask the breeder to give you a rag or towel that has been in the puppy's nest and thus carries a familiar scent. The first few nights in its new home will be strange and frightening and it will certainly make itself heard. The familiar towel, a ticking alarm clock under its blanket and a warm hot-water bottle will possibly help it feel that it's not alone. However, if your puppy does whine, under no circumstances go to it. If you do, your puppy will feel its behaviour has been rewarded, and its whining will only get worse. If you stay consistent, it will stop after a few nights.

Travelling with your Dobermann

There are a few things to think about before travelling with your dog. While one dog may enjoy travelling, another may hate it. You may like holidays in far-away places, but it's questionable whether your dog will enjoy them as much.

That very first trip

The first trip of a puppy's life is also the most nerve-wracking. This is the trip from the breeder's to its new home. Preferably pick up your puppy in the early morning. It then has the whole day to get used to its new situation. Ask the breeder not to feed it that day. The young animal will be overwhelmed by all kinds of new experiences. Firstly, it's away from its mother; it's in a small room (the car) with all its different smells, noises and strange people. So there's a big chance that the puppy will be car-sick this first time, with the annoying consequence that it will remember travelling in the car as an unpleasant experience.

So it's important to make this first trip as pleasant as possible. When picking up a puppy, always take someone with you who can sit in the back seat with the puppy on his or her lap and talk to it calmly. If it's too warm for the puppy, a place on the floor at the feet of your companion is ideal. The pup will lie there relatively quietly and may even take a nap. Ask the breeder for a cloth or something else from the puppies basket or bed that carries a familiar scent. The puppy can lie on this in the car, and it will also help if it feels lonely during the first nights at home.

If the trip home is a long one, then stop for a break (once in a while). Let your puppy roam and sniff around (on the lead!), offer it a little drink and, if necessary, do its business. Do take care to lay an old towel in the car. It can happen that the puppy, in its nervousness, may urinate or be sick. It's also good advice to give a puppy positive experiences with car journeys. Make short trips to nice places where you can walk and play with it. It can be a real nuisance if your dog doesn't like travelling in a car. After all, once in a while you will have to take it to certain places, such as the vet's or to visit friends and acquaintances.

Taking your Dobermann on holiday

When making holiday plans, you also need to think about what you're going to do with your dog during that time. Are you taking it with you, putting it into kennels or leaving it with friends? In any event there are a number of things you need to do in good time. If you want to take your dog with you, you need to be sure in advance that it will be welcome at your holiday home, and what rules there are. If you're going abroad it will need certain vaccinations and a health certificate, which normally need to be done four weeks before departure. You must also be sure that you've made all the arrangements necessary to bring your dog back home to the UK, without it needing to go into quarantine under the rabies regulations. Your vet can give you the most recent information.

If your trip is to southern Europe, ask for a treatment against tics

(you can read more about this in the chapter on parasites).

Although dog-owners usually enjoy taking their dog on holiday, you must seriously ask yourself whether the dog feels that way too. Dobermanns certainly don't always feel comfortable in a hot country. Days spent travelling in a car are also often not their preference, and some dogs suffer badly from car-sickness. There are good medicines for this, but it's questionable whether you're doing your dog a favour with them. If you do decide to take it with you, make regular stops at safe places during your journey, so that your dog can have a good run. Take plenty of fresh drinking water with you, as well as the food your dog is used to. Don't leave your dog in the car that is standing in the sun. It can quickly be overcome by the heat, with even fatal consequences. If you can't avoid it, park the car in the shade if at all possible, and leave a window open for a little fresh air. Even if you've taken these precautions, never stay away long!

If you're travelling by plane or ship, make your travel plands in time to ensure that your dog can travel with you and that the necessary rules are observed. You will need some time to make all the

arrangements. Should you decide not to take your dog with you, and you then need to find somewhere for it to stay. Arrangements for a place in kennels need to be made well in advance, and there may be certain vaccinations required, which need to be given a minimum of one month before the stay.

If your dog can't be accommodated in the homes of relatives or friends, it might be possible to have an acquaintance stay in your house. This also needs to be arranged well in advance, as it may be difficult to find someone who can do this.

Always ensure that your dog can be traced should it run away or get lost while on holiday. A little tube with your address or a tag with home and holiday address can prevent a lot of problems.

Moving home

Dogs generally become more attached to humans than to the house they live in. Moving home is usually not a problem for them. But it can be useful before moving to let the dog get to know its new home and the area around it.

If you can, leave your dog with relatives or friends (or in kennels) on the day of the move. The chance of it running away or getting lost is then practically non-existent. When your move is complete, you can pick up your dog and let it quietly get familiar with its new home and environment. Give it its own place in the house at once and it will quickly adapt. During the first week or so, always walk your dog on a lead because an animal can also get lost in new surroundings. Always take a different route so it quickly gets to know the neighbourhood.

Don't forget to get your new address and phone number engraved on the dog's tag. Send a change of address notice to the chip or tattoo registration office. Dogs must sometimes be registered in a new community.

Feeding your Dobermann

A dog will actually eat a lot more than just meat. In the wild it would eat its prey complete with skin and fur, including the bones, stomach, and the innards with their semi-digested vegetable material.

In this way the dog supplements its meat menu with the vitamins and minerals it needs. This is also the basis for feeding a domestic dog

Ready-made foods

It's not easy for a layman to put together a complete menu for a dog, that includes all the necessary proteins, fats, vitamins and minerals in just the right proportions and quantities. Meat alone is certainly not a complete meal for a dog. It contains too little calcium. A calcium deficiency over time will lead to bone defects, and for a fast-growing puppy this can lead to serious skeletal deformities.

If you mix its food yourself, you can easily give your dog too much in terms of vitamins and minerals, which can also be bad for your dog's health. You can avoid these problems by giving it ready-made food of a good brand. These products are well-balanced and contain everything your dog needs. Supplements such as vitamin preparations are superfluous. The amount of food your dog needs depends on its weight and activity level. You can find guidelines on the packaging. Split the food into two meals per day if possible, and always ensure there's a bowl of fresh drinking water next to its food.

Give your dog the time to digest its food, don't let it outside straight after a meal. A dog should also never play on a full stomach. This can cause stomach torsion, (the stomach turning over), which can be fatal for your dog.

Because the nutritional needs of a dog depend, among other things, on its age and way of life, there are many different types of dog food available. There are "light" foods for less active dogs, "energy" foods for working dogs and "senior" foods for the older dog.

Puppy chunks

There is now a wide assortment of puppy chunks on the market. These chunks contain a higher content of growth-promoting nutrients, such as protein and calcium. For large breeds such as the Dobermann however, these chunks can actually be harmful. The dog will grow fast enough, and faster growth will only promote conditions such as hip and elbow dysplasia (See the chapter Your Dobermann's health). Give your puppy only special puppy chunks for larger breeds.

Canned foods, mixer and dry foods

Ready-made foods available at pet shops or in the supermarket can roughly be split into canned food, mixer and dry food. Whichever form you choose, ensure that it's a complete food with all the necessary ingredients. You can see this on the packaging.

Most dogs love canned food. Although the better brands are composed well, they do have one disadvantage: they are soft. A dog fed only on canned food will sooner or later have problems with its teeth (plaque, paradontosis). Besides canned food, give your dog hard foods at certain times or a dog chew, such as Nylabone Healthy Edibles.

Mixer is a food consisting of chunks, dried vegetables and grains. Almost all moisture has been extracted. The advantages of mixer are that it is light and keeps well. You add a certain amount of water and the meal is ready. A disadvantage is that it must definitely not be fed without water. Without the extra fluid, mixer will absorb the fluids present in the stomach, with serious results. Should your dog manage to get at the bag and enjoy its contents, you must immediately give it plenty to drink.

Dry chunks have also had the moisture extracted but not as much as mixer. The advantage of dry foods is that they are hard, forcing the dog to use its jaws, removing plaque and massaging the gums.

Dog chew products

Of course, once in a while you want to spoil your dog with something extra. Don't give it pieces of cheese or sausage as these contain too much salt and fat.
There are various products available that a dog will find delicious and which are also healthy, especially for its teeth. You'll find a

large range of varying quality in the pet shop.

The butcher's left-overers

The bones of slaughtered animals have traditionally been given to the dog, and dogs love them, but they are not without risks. Pork and poultry bones are too weak. They can splinter and cause serious injury to the intestines. Beef bones are more suitable, but they must first be cooked to kill off dangerous bacteria.
Pet shops carry a range of smoked, cooked and dried abattoir residue, such as pigs' ears, bull penis, tripe sticks, oxtails, gullet, dried muscle meat, and hoof chews.

Fresh meat

If you do want to give your dog fresh meat occasionally, never give it raw, but always boiled or roasted. Raw (or not fully cooked) pork or chicken can contain life-threatening bacteria. Chicken can be contaminated by the notorious salmonella bacteria, while pork can carry the Aujeszky virus. This disease is incurable and will quickly lead to the death of your pet.

Buffalo or cowhide chews

Dog chews are mostly made of beef or buffalo hide. Chews are usually knotted or pressed hide and can come in the form of little shoes, twisted sticks, lollies, balls and various other shapes; nice to look at and a nice change.

Munchy sticks

Munchy sticks are green, yellow, red or brown coloured sticks of various thicknesses. They consist of ground buffalo hide with a number of often undefined additives. The composition and quality of these between-meal treats is not always clear. Some are fine, but there have also been sticks found to contain high levels of cardboard and even paint residues. Choose a product whose ingredients are clearly described.

Overweight?

Recent investigations have shown that many dogs are overweight. A dog usually gets too fat because of

over-feeding and lack of exercise. Use of medicines or a disease is rarely the cause. Dogs that get too fat are often given too much food or treats between meals. Gluttony or boredom can also be a cause, and a dog often puts on weight following castration or sterilisation. Due to changes in hormone levels, it becomes less active and consumes less energy. Finally, simply too little exercise alone can lead to a dog becoming overweight.

You can use the following rule of thumb to check whether your dog is overweight: you should be able to feel its ribs, but not see them. If you can't feel its ribs then your dog is much too fat. Overweight dogs live a passive life, they play too little and tire quickly. They also suffer from all kinds of medical problems (problems in joints and heart conditions). They usually die younger too.
So it's important to make sure your dog doesn't get too fat. Always follow the guidelines on food packaging. Adapt them if your dog is less active or gets lots of snacks. Try to make sure your dog gets plenty of exercise by playing and running with it as much as you can. If your dog starts to show signs of putting on weight you can switch to a low-calorie food. If it's really too fat and reducing its food quantity doesn't help, then a special diet is the only solution.

Caring for your Dobermann

Good (daily) care is extremely important for your dog. A well-cared for dog is less likely to become ill. Caring for your dog is not only necessary but also a pleasure.

Master and dog are giving each other some attention, and it's an excellent opportunity for a game and a cuddle.

The coat

Caring for your dog's coat involves regular brushing and combing, together with checking for parasites such as fleas. How often a dog needs to be brushed and combed depends on the length of its coat. A good brush with a rubber brush or glove once or twice a week is usually enough to keep a Dobermann's coat in peak condition. Its coat will take on a splendid gloss if you rub it down with a damp shammy leather or velvet cloth after brushing. During the moulting period, you can help your dog to replace its coat especially quickly by brushing it every day. Use the right equipment for grooming. Combs should not be too sharp and you should use a rubber or natural hairbrush. Always comb from the head back towards the tail, following the direction of the hair.

If you get a puppy used to being brushed from an early age, it will enjoy having its coat cared for. Only bath a dog when it's really necessary. Always use a special dog shampoo and make sure it doesn't get into the dog's eyes or ears. Rinse the suds out thoroughly.

A vet can prescribe special medicinal shampoos for some skin conditions. Always follow the instructions to the letter. Good flea prevention is highly important to avoid skin and coat problems.

Fleas must be treated not only on the dog itself but also in its surroundings (see the chapter on parasites). Coat problems can also occur due to an allergy to certain food substances. In such cases, a vet can prescribe a hypo-allergenic diet.

Teeth

A dog must be able to eat properly to stay in good condition, so it needs healthy teeth. Check its teeth regularly. Get in touch with your vet if you suspect that all is not well. Regular feeds of hard dry food can help keep your dogs teeth clean and healthy. There are special dog chews, such as Nylabone, on the market that help prevent plaque and help keep the animal's breath fresh.
What really helps is regular tooth brushing. You can use special tooth-brushes for dogs, but a finger wrapped in a small piece of gauze will also do the job. Get your dog used to having its teeth cleaned at an early age and you won't have problems.

You can even teach an older dog to have its teeth cleaned. With a dog chew as a reward it will certainly be happy.

Nails

On a dog that regularly walks on hard surfaces, its nails usually grind themselves down. In this case there's no need to clip their nails. But it wouldn't do any harm to check their length now and again, especially on dogs that don't get out on the streets often. Using a piece of paper, you can easily see whether its nails are too long. If you can push the paper between the nail and the ground when the dog is standing, then the nail is the right length.

Nails that are too long can bother a dog. It can injure itself when scratching, so they must be kept trimmed. You can buy special nail clippers in pet shops. Be careful not to clip back too far as you could damage the skin around the nail, which can bleed profusely. If you feel unsure, have this necessary task done by a vet or an animal beauty parlour.

Special attention is needed for the extra nail on the inside of the rear paws, the so-called dewclaw. Clip this nail back regularly, otherwise it can get caught on it and become damaged.

Eyes

A dog's eyes should be cleaned regularly. Discharge gets into the corners of the eye. You can easily remove them by wiping them downward with your thumb. If you don't like doing that, use a piece of tissue or toilet paper.

Keeping your dog's eyes clean will take only a few seconds a day, so do it every day. If the discharge becomes yellow this could point to an irritation or infection. Eye drops (from your vet) will quickly solve this problem.

Ears

The ears are often forgotten when caring for dogs, but they must be checked at least once a week. If its ears are very dirty or have too much wax, you must clean them. This should preferably be done with a clean cotton cloth, moistened with lukewarm water or baby oil. Cotton wool is not suitable due to the fluff it can leave behind. NEVER penetrate the ear canal with an object. If you do neglect cleaning your dog's ears there's a substantial risk of infection. A dog that is constantly scratching at its ears might be suffering from dirty ears, an ear infection or ear mites, making a visit to the vet essential.

Bringing up your Dobermann

It is very important that your dog is properly brought up and is obedient. Not only will this bring you more pleasure, but it's also nicer for your environment.

A puppy can learn what it may and may not do by playing. Rewards and consistency are important tools in bringing up a dog. Reward it with your voice, a stroke or something tasty and it will quickly learn to obey. A puppy-training course can also help you along the way.

(Dis)obedience

A dog that won't obey you is not just a problem for you, but also for your surroundings. It's therefore important to avoid unwanted behaviour. In fact, this is what training your dog is all about, so get started early. 'Start 'em young!' applies to dogs too. An untrained dog is not just a nuisance, but can also cause dangerous situations, running into the road, chasing joggers or jumping at people. A dog must be trained out of this undesirable behaviour as quickly as possible. The longer you let it go on, the more difficult it will become to correct. The best thing to do is to attend a special obedience course. This won't only help to correct the dog's behaviour, but its owner also learns how to handle undesirable behaviour at home. A dog must not only obey its master during training, but at home too.

Always be consistent when training good behaviour and correcting annoying behaviour. This means a dog may always behave in a certain way, or must never behave that way. Reward it for good behaviour and never punish it after the fact for any wrongdoing. If your dog finally comes after you've been calling it a long time, then reward it. If you're angry because you had to wait so long, it may feel it's actually being punished for coming. It will probably not obey at all the next time for fear of punishment.

Try to take no notice of undesirable behaviour. Your dog will perceive your reaction (even a negative one) as a reward for this behaviour. If you need to correct the dog, then do this immediately. Use your voice or grip it by the scruff of its neck and push it to the ground. This is the way a mother dog calls her pups to order. Rewards for good behaviour are, by far, preferable to punishment; they always get a better result.

House-training

The very first training (and one of the most important) that a dog needs is house-training. The basis for good house-training is keeping a good eye on your puppy. If you pay attention, you will notice that it will sniff a long time and turns around a certain spot before doing its business there. Pick it up gently and place it outside, always at the same place. Reward it abundantly if it does its business there.

Another good moment for house-training is after eating or sleeping. A puppy often needs to do its business at these times. Let it relieve itself before playing with it, otherwise it will forget to do so and you'll not reach your goal. For the first few days, take your puppy out for a walk just after it's eaten or woken up. It will quickly learn the meaning, especially if it's rewarded with a dog biscuit for a successful attempt. Of course, it's not always possible to go out after every snack or snooze. Lay newspapers at different spots in the house. Whenever the pup needs to do its business, place it on a newspaper. After some time it will start to look for a place itself. Then start to reduce the number of newspapers until there is just one left, at the front or back door. The puppy will learn to go to the door if it needs to relieve itself. Then you put it on the lead and go out with it. Finally you can remove the last newspaper. Your puppy is now house-trained.

One thing that certainly won't work is punishing an accident after the fact. A dog whose nose is rubbed in its urine or its droppings won't understand that at all. It will only get frightened of you. Rewarding works much better than punishment. An indoor kennel or cage can be a good tool to help in house-training. A puppy won't foul its own nest, so a kennel can be a good solution for the night, or during periods in the day when you can't watch it. But a kennel must not become a prison where your dog is locked up day and night.

Basis obedience

The basic commands for an obedient dog are those for sit, lie down, come and stay. But a puppy should first learn its name. Use it as much as possible from the first day on followed by a friendly 'Come!' Reward it with your voice and a stroke when it comes to you. Your puppy will quickly recognise the intention and has now learned its first command in a playful manner. Don't be too harsh with a young puppy, and don't always punish it immediately if it doesn't always react in the right way. When you call your puppy to you in this way have it come right to you. You can teach a pup to sit by holding a piece of dog biscuit above his nose and then slowly moving it backwards. The puppy's head will also move backwards until its hind legs slowly go down. At that moment you call 'Sit!' After a few attempts, it will quickly know this nice game. Use the 'Sit!' command before giving your dog its food, putting it on the lead, or before it's allowed to cross the road.

Teaching the command to lie down is similar. Instead of moving the piece of dog biscuit backwards, move it down vertically until your hand reaches the ground and then forwards. The dog will also move its forepaws forwards and lie down on its own. At that moment call 'Lie down!' This command is useful when you want a dog to be quiet.

Two people are needed for the 'Come!' command. One holds the dog back while the other runs away. After about fifteen metres, he stops and enthusiastically calls 'Come!' The other person now lets the dog go, and it should obey the command at once. Again you reward it abundantly. The 'Come!' command is useful in many situations and good for safety too. A dog learns to stay from the sitting or lying position. While its sitting or lying down, you give the command: 'Stay!' and then step back one step. If the dog moves with you, quietly put it back in position, without displaying anger. If you do react angrily, you're actually punishing it for coming to you, and you'll only confuse your dog. It can't understand that coming is rewarded one time, and punished another. Once the dog stays nicely reward it abundantly. Practice this exercise with increasing distances (at first no more than one metre). The 'Stay!' command is useful when getting out of the car.

Courses

Obedience courses to help you bring up your dog are available across the country. These courses are not just informative, but also fun for dog and master.

With a puppy, you can begin with a puppy course. This is designed to provide the basic training. A puppy that has attended such a course has learned about all kinds of things that will confront it in later life: other dogs, humans, traffic and what these mean. The puppy will also learn obedience and to follow a number of basic commands. Apart from all that, attention will be given to important subjects such as brushing, being alone, travelling in a car, and doing its business in the right places.

The next step after a puppy course is a course for young dogs. This course repeats the basic exercises and ensures that the growing dog doesn't learns bad habits. After this, the dog can move on to an obedience course for full-grown dogs. For more information on where to find courses in your area, contact your local kennel club. You can get its address from the Kennel Club of Great Britain in London. In some areas, the RSPCA organises obedience classes and your local branch may be able to give you information.

Play and toys

There are various ways to play with your dog, You can romp and run with it, but also play a number of games, such as retrieving, tug-of-war, hide-and-seek and catch. A tennis ball is ideal for retrieving, you can play tug-of-war with an old sock or a special tugging rope. Start with tug-of-war only when your dog is a year old. A puppy must first get its second teeth and then they need several months to strengthen. There's a real chance of your dog's teeth becoming deformed if you start too young. You can use almost anything for a game of hide-and-seek. A frisbee is ideal for catching games. Never use too small a ball for games. It can easily get lodged into the dog's throat.
Play is extremely important. Not only does it strengthen the bond between dog and master, but it's

also healthy for both. Make sure that you're the one that ends the game. Only stop when the dog has brought back the ball or frisbee, and make sure you always win the tug-of-war. This confirms your dominant position in the hierarchy. Use these toys only during play so that the dog doesn't forget their significance. When choosing a special dog toy, remember that dogs are hardly careful with them. So always buy toys of good quality that a dog can't easily destroy.

Be very careful with sticks and twigs. The latter, particularly, can easily splinter. A splinter of wood in your dog's throat or intestines can cause awful problems. Throwing sticks or twigs can also be dangerous. If they stick into the ground a dog can easily run into them with an open mouth. If you would like to do more than just play games, you can now also play sports with your dog. For people who want to do more, there are various other sporting alternatives such as flyball, agility, and obedience.

Aggression

A properly socialised and rigorously brought-up Dobermann is practically never aggressive. But even they can sometimes be difficult with other animals or people, so it's good to understand more about the background of aggression in dogs.

There are two different types of aggressive behaviour: The anxious-aggressive dog and the dominant-aggressive dog. An anxious-aggressive dog can be recognised by its pulled back ears and its low position. It will have pulled in its lips, showing its teeth. This dog is aggressive because it's very frightened and feels cornered. It would prefer to run away, but if it can't then it will bite to defend itself. It will grab its victim anywhere it can. The attack is usually brief and, as soon as the dog can see a way to escape, it's gone. In a confrontation with other dogs, it will normally turn out as the loser. It can become even more aggressive once it's realised that people or other dogs are afraid of it. This behaviour cannot be corrected just like that. First you have to try and understand what the dog is afraid of. Professional advice is a good idea here because the wrong approach can easily make the problem worse.

The dominant-aggressive dog's body language is different. Its ears stand up and its tail is raised and stiff. This dog will always go for its victim's arms, legs or throat. It is extremely self-assured and highly placed in the dog hierarchy. Its attack is a display of power rather than a consequence of fear. This dog needs to know who's boss. You must bring it up rigorously and with a strong hand. An obedience course can help.

A dog may also bite itself because it's in pain. This is a natural defensive reaction. In this case try to resolve the dog's fear as far as possible. Reward him for letting you get to the painful spot. Be careful, because a dog in pain may also bite its master! Muzzling it can help prevent problems if you have to do something that may be painful. Never punish a dog for this type of aggression!

Fear

The source of anxious behaviour can often be traced to the first weeks of a dog's life. A shortage of new experiences during this important phase (also called the 'socialisation phase') has great influence on its later behaviour. A dog that never encountered humans, other dogs or animals during the socialisation phase will be afraid of them later. This fear is common in dogs brought up in a barn or kennel, with almost no contact with humans. As we saw, fear can lead to aggressive behaviour, so it's important that a puppy gets as many new impressions as possible in the first weeks of its life. Take it with you into town in the car or on the bus, walk it down busy streets and allow it to have plenty of contact with people, other dogs and other animals.

It's a huge task to turn an anxious, poorly socialised dog into a real pet. It will probably take an enormous amount of attention, love, patience and energy to get such an animal used to everything around it. Reward it often and give it plenty of time to adapt and, over time, it will learn to trust you and become less anxious. Try not to force anything, because that will always have the reverse effect. Here too, an obedience course can help a lot. A dog can be especially afraid of strangers. Have visitors give it something tasty as a treat. Put a can of dog cookies by the door so that your visitors can spoil your dog when they arrive. Here again, don't try to force anything. If the dog is still frightened, leave it in peace.

Dogs are often frightened in certain situations; well-known examples are thunderstorms and fireworks. In these cases try to ignore their anxious behaviour. If you react to their whimpering and whining, it's the same as rewarding it. If you ignore its fear completely, the dog will quickly learn that nothing is wrong. You can speed up this 'learning process' by rewarding its positive behaviour.

Rewarding

Rewarding forms the basis for bringing up a dog. Rewarding good behaviour works far better than punishing bad behaviour and rewarding is also much more fun. Recently, the opinions on upbringing for dogs have gradually changed. In the past the proper way to correct bad behaviour was regarded as a sharp pull on the lead. Today, experts view rewards as a positive incentive to get dogs to do what we expect of them. There are many ways to reward a dog. The usual ways are a stroke or a friendly word, even without a tasty treat to go with it. Of course, a piece of dog biscuit does wonders when you're training a puppy. Be sure you always have something delicious in your pocket to reward good behaviour. Another form of reward is play. Whenever a dog notices you have a ball in your pocket, it won't go far from your side. As soon as you've finished playing, put the ball away. This way your dog will always do its best in exchange for a game. Despite the emphasis you put on rewarding good behaviour, a dog can sometimes be a nuisance or disobedient. You must correct such behaviour immediately. Always be consistent: once 'no', always'no'.

Barking

Dogs which bark too much and too often are a nuisance for their surroundings. A dog-owner may tolerate barking up to a point, but neighbours are often annoyed by the unnecessary noise. Don't encourage your puppy to bark and yelp. Of course, it should be able to announce its presence, but if it goes on barking it must be called to order with a strict 'Quiet!'. If a puppy fails to obey, just hold its muzzle closed with your hand.

A dog will sometimes bark for long periods when left alone. It feels threatened and tries to get someone's attention by barking. There are special training programmes for this problem, where dogs learn that being alone is nothing to be afraid of, and that its master will always return.

You can practice this with your dog at home. Leave the room and come back in at once. Reward your dog if it stays quiet. Gradually increase the length of your absences and keep rewarding it as long as it remains quiet. Never punish the dog if it does bark or yelp. It will never understand punishment afterwards, and this will only make the problem worse. Never go back into the room as long as your dog is barking, as it will view this as a reward. You might want to make the dog feel more comfortable by switching the radio on for company during your absence. It will eventually learn that you always come back and the barking will reduce. If you don't get the required result, attend an obedience course.

Walking on the lead

It is important that your dog walks properly on the lead. Walking a powerful Dobermann that pulls on its lead, or walks irregularly, can be very tiring! Learning to follow off the lead is too difficult for a puppy, so begin with a few walks on the lead. It is recommended that your dog follow you on your left. The left is the usual side used in training courses that you might want to take part in with your dog later. Of course, you can also use the right-hand side, as long as you stay consistent. Otherwise your dog may get confused, and forming habits is very important for a dog. Start teaching your dog to walk on the lead by putting on a soft-leather, not too narrow, collar and leave it on for a few days. At the beginning, the puppy will probably try to pull this off, but over time it will get used to it automatically.

Try to start practising during the day in a quiet place. Make it a habit for your puppy to do its business first, so let it free for a while so that it can play. Then it will have let off some steam and will be better able to concentrate on its training. Always try to get your dog to sit quietly beside you before letting it loose, but don't force this. After all, learning everything at once is a tall order. Hold your puppy by the collar, release the lead, wait a moment and than call its name followed by the command "Run!" in an inviting way. Then run a few steps with it before letting it free. Your puppy must now be allowed to go its own way for the time you've allowed. Let it investigate everything, run and dig to its heart's content. Doing things on its own initiative can only help your dog's development.

After playing, it's time for your puppy to 'go to work'. At first it won't think much of having to walk with you. As soon as it feels the resistance of the lead on its collar, it will lie down, sit or try anything it can to get out of the collar. Get down on your haunches, call your puppy by its name in a friendly manner and carefully pull the lead towards you. Your puppy will soon give up its protest, and has now established the link that walking with its master is something pleasurable.

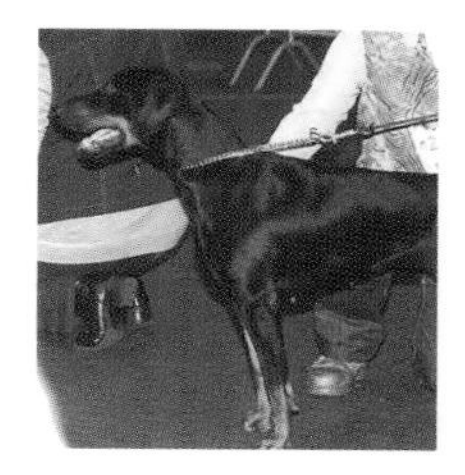

Dogs usually run happily to the door as soon as their master picks up their lead, but sometimes, perhaps, your puppy might not feel like going out. If it refuses to walk with you, give it a gentle tug on the lead. Never drag it because this can be bad for its joints and it will only find walking on the lead an unpleasant event. This will act against you if you want your dog to walk properly later.

Once a puppy has mastered walking on the lead, and understands there's no point in refusing to go, then it will try another trick. It will start to pull at the lead. You can correct this too with short tugs on the lead and the commando 'heel!' or 'better!'. Whatever commands you choose is completely up to you, but keep them short and never change them again. Make sure different commands don't sound alike; a dog responds to a sound, and not to what you say.

Once walking goes well in quiet streets, then look for a busier area. Keep the exercises short for the

time being. Five intensive minutes with your puppy are enough. Stay calm and praise it. Your voice is a great support in any situation.

Now it's time to cross the 't's and dot the 'i's. Shorten the lead until your dog's head is parallel with your knees. If it stays back or pulls forward too much, give it a little tug on the lead with the command 'heel!' or 'better!'. When this is going well, you losen the lead out again, but keep correcting as soon as your pup makes a mistake.

With the necessary patience and perseverance, you will have your dog walking properly beside you on the lead at six months. You should not expect any more than that. Many dogs are entered for certain courses because their master wants a result too fast. Wait a month or so longer before training a certain aspect rather than getting half the result too fast. Trying to force the dog will also only achieve the opposite to what you want. The dog will notice that you're not relaxed. This will only cause negative emotions, whereby you'll only get a result with difficulty, if at all.

Chasing cats

Of course, it's funny watching a young puppy in full chase behind a cat, but you must try to suppress these instincts from the beginning. This is also very important for any courses you might want to follow with it later. A young dog must learn to control its hunting instincts. If it's now allowed to chase the chickens or the neighbour's cat, it will later chase anything that tries to escape from it. Ideally, you should get a kitten at the same time as your puppy and let them grow up together. Your dog will then be used to cats and won't regard them as a natural enemy. It's a common misnomer that dogs and cats can't get along with each other.

Never make the mistake of provoking or waking your puppy's assumed aggression towards cats. You are creating a problem that in fact does not exist. If your dog does react by standing tensely when it sees a cat, be firm. Reprimand it and use your strictest command. This is an example of a moment when you must demonstrate your authority!

It will generally help life in general if you react totally neutral to other animals, especially cats that your dog may be confronted with around town. Be rigorous from the first day on and never allow your dog to chase another animal. Once it has learned to lie quietly later, it will remain so and observe other animals without moving.

Breeding

Dogs, and thus Dobermanns, follow their instincts, and reproduction is one of nature's important processes.

For people who enjoy breeding dogs this is a positive circumstance. Those who simply want a cosy companion' however, do not need the regular adventures with females on heat and unrestrainable. Knowing a little about breeding in dogs will help you to understand why they behave the way they do, and the measures you need to take when this happens.

Liability

Breeding dogs is much more than simply 1+1= many. If you're planning to breed with your Dobermann, be on your guard, otherwise the whole affair can turn into a financial drama because, under the law, a breeder is liable for the 'quality' of his puppies.

The breeder clubs place strict conditions on animals used for breding. They must be examined for possible congenital defects (see the chapter Your Dobermann's health). This is the breeder's first obligation, and if you breed a litter and sell the puppies without these checks having been made, you may be held liable by the new owners for any costs arising from any inherited defects. These (veterinary) costs can be enormous! So contact the breed association if you plan to breed a litter of Dobermanns.

The female in season

Bitches become sexually mature at about eight to twelve months. Then they go into season for the first time. They are 'on heat' for two to three weeks. During this period they discharge little drops of blood and they are very attractive to males. The bitch is fertile during the second half of her season, and will accept a male to mate. The best time for mating is then between the ninth and thirteenth day of her season. A female's first season is often shorter and less severe than those that follow. If you do want to breed with your female you must allow this first (and sometimes the second) season to pass. Most bitches go into season twice per year. If you do plan to breed with your Dobermann in the future, then sterilisation is not an option to prevent unwanted offspring. A temporary solution is a contraceptive injection, although this is controversial because of side effects such as womb infections.

Phantom pregnancy

A phantom pregnancy is a not an uncommon occurrence. The female behaves as if she has a litter. She takes all kinds of things to her basket and treats them like puppies. Her teats swell and sometimes milk is actually produced. The female will sometimes behave aggressively towards people or other animals, as if she is defending her young. Phantom pregnancies usually begin two months after a season and can last a number of weeks. If it happens to a bitch once, it will often then occur after every season. If she suffers under it, sterilisation is the best solution, because continual phantom pregnancies increase the risk of womb or teat conditions. In the short term a hormone treatment is worth trying, perhaps also homeopathic medicines. Camphor spirit can give relief when teats are heavily swollen, but rubbing the teats with ice or a cold cloth (moisten and freeze) can also help relieve the pain. Feed the female less than usual, and makes sure she gets enough attraction and extra exercise.

Preparing to breed

If you do plan to breed a litter of puppies, you must first wait for your female to be physically and mentally full-grown. In any event you must let her first season pass. To mate a bitch, you need a male. You could simply let her out on the street and she will quickly return home pregnant. But if you have a pure-bred Dobermann, then it certainly makes sense to mate her with the best possible candidate, even if she has no pedigree. Proceed with caution and think especially about the following: Accompanying a bitch through pregnancy, birth and the first eight to twelve weeks afterwards is a time consuming affair. Never breed with Dobermanns that have congenital defects and this also applies to dogs without papers. The same goes for hyperactive, nervous and shy dogs. If your Dobermann does have a pedigree, then mate her with a dog that also has one. For more information, contact your local breed club secretary.

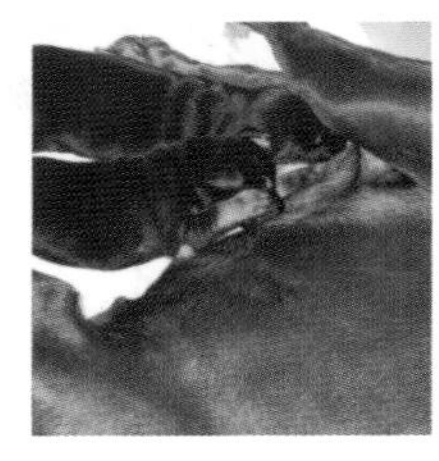

Pregnancy

It's often difficult to tell at first when a bitch is pregnant. Only after about four weeks can you feel the pups in her womb. She will now slowly get fatter and her behaviour will usually change. Her teats will swell during the last few weeks of pregnancy. The average pregnancy lasts 63 days, and costs her a lot of energy. In the beginning she is fed her normal amount of food, but her nutritional needs increase in jumps during the second half of the pregnancy. Give her approximately fifteen percent more food each week from the fifth week on. The mother-to-be needs extra energy and proteins during this phase of her pregnancy. During the last weeks you can give her a concentrated food, rich in energy, such as dry puppy food. Divide this into several small portions per day, because she can no longer deal with large portions of food. Towards the end of the pregnancy, her energy needs can easily be one-and-a-half times more than usual.

After about seven weeks the mother will start to demonstrate nesting behaviour and starts to look for a place to give birth to her puppies. This might be her own basket or a special whelping box. This must be ready at least a week before the birth to give the mother

time to get used to it. The basket or box should preferably be in a quiet place.

The birth

The average litter is between three and nine puppies. The birth usually passes without problems. Of course, you must contact your vet immediately if you suspect a problem!

Suckling

After birth, the mother starts to produce milk. The suckling period is very demanding. During the first three to four weeks the pups rely entirely on their mother's milk. During this time she needs extra food and fluids. This can be up to three or four times the normal amount. If she's producing too little milk, you can give both mother and her young special puppy milk. Here too, divide the high quantity of food the mother needs over several smaller portions. Again, choose a concentrated, high-energy, food and give her plenty of fresh drinking water, but not cow's milk, which can cause diarrhoea.

You can give the puppies some supplemental solid food when they are three to four weeks old. There are special puppy foods available that follow on well from the mother's milk and can easily be eaten with their milk teeth.

Ideally, the puppies are fully weaned, at an age of six or seven weeks i.e. they no longer drink their mother's milk. The mother's milk production gradually stops and her food needs also drop. Within a couple of weeks after weaning, the mother should again be getting the same amount of food as before the pregnancy.

Castration and sterilisation

As soon as you are sure your bitch should never bear a (new) litter, a sterilisation is the best solution. During sterilisation the uterus is removed in an operation. The bitch no longer goes into season and can never become pregnant. The best age for a sterilisation is about eighteen months, when the bitch is more or less fully-grown.

A male dog is usually only castrated for medical reasons or to correct undesirable sexual behaviour. During a castration the testicles are removed, which is a simple procedure and usually without complications. There is no special age for castration but, where possible, wait until the dog is fully-grown. Vasectomy is sufficient where it's only a case of making the dog infertile. In this case the dog keeps its sexual drive but can no longer reproduce.

Sport and shows

A Dobermann is a real working dog and was not born to lay around. It will be a true companion that you can while away the hours with as long as you do enough with it. This chapter can only offer a brief look at all the possibilities. The breed club can give you more information.

In Europe the Dobermann is used as a working dog

Exhibitions and exemption shows

Visiting a dog show is a pleasant experience for both dog and master, and for some dog-lovers it is an intensive hobby. They visit countless shows every year. Others find it nice to visit an exemption show with their dog just once. It's worth making the effort to visit an exemption show where a judge's experienced eyes will inspect your Dobermann and assess it for form, gait, condition and behaviour. The judge's report will teach you your dog's weak and strong points, which may help you when choosing a mate for breeding. You can also exchange experiences with other Dobermann owners. Official dog shows are only open to dogs with a pedigree.

Ring training and club events

If you've never been to a dog show, you will probably be fumbling in the dark in terms of what will be expected of you and your dog. Many Dobermann and general dog clubs organise so-called ring training courses for dogs going to a show for the first time. This training teaches you exactly what the judge will be looking for, and you can practice this together with your dog.

Open shows

All dog clubs organise dog shows. You must enter your dog in advance in a certain class. These metings are usually small and friendly and are often the first acquaintance dog and master makes with a "real" judge. This is an overwhelming experience for your dog -

a lot of its contemporaries and a strange man or woman who fiddles around with it and peers into its mouth. After a few times, your dog will know exactly what's expected of it and will happily go to the next club match.

Championship shows

Various championship shows take place during the course of the year with different prizes. These shows are much more strictly organised than club matches. Your dog must be registered in a certain class in advance and it will then be listed in a catalogue. On the day itself, the dog is usually kept on a bench until its turn comes up. During the judging in the ring, it's important that you show your dog at its best. The judge examines each dog in turn. When all the dogs from that class have been judged, the best are selected and placed. After all the judging for is finished all the winners of the various classes in that sex they compete for the Challenge Certificate in that sex. (3 Challenge certificates from different judges, and your Dobermann will be a Champion in the UK.) The best Dobermann in the eyes of the judge gets this award. Finally, the winners of each sex compete for the title of Best in Show. Of course, your dog must look very smart for the show. The judge will not be impressed if its coat is not clean or is tangled, and its paws are dirty. Nails must be clipped and teeth free of plaque. The dog must also be free of parasites and ailments. A bitch must not be in season and a male must be in possession of both testicles. Apart from those things, judges also hate badly brought-up, anxious or nervous dogs. Get in touch with your local dog club or the breed association if you want to know more about shows.

Don't forget!

If you're planning to take your dog to a club match or in fact to any show, you need to be well prepared. Don't forget the following:

For yourself:

- Show documents if they have been sent to you
- Food and drink
- Clip for the catalogue number
- Chairs if an outside show

For your dog:

- Food and water bowls and food
- Dog blanket and perhaps a cushion
- Show lead
- A brush
- A benching chain and collar

Sport and work

Enthusiasts can actively work with their Dobermann in many other ways. From tracking to sports, the possibilities are endless.

Agility

Agility is a form of sport that reinforces the contact between man and dog. Because there are no strict requirements in terms of signals and commands, it's more a matter of harmony between dog and master, and combinations with high levels of mutual understanding often score the highest marks. The dog must go around a course with various obstacles (see-saw, slalom, tunnel). On the one hand, agility looks spectacular and actually quite simple. The master can use as many signals and commands he feels necessary. But just that fact makes agility more difficult than it appears. The more you can do, the more can go wrong.

Traffic-training

All Dobermanns that want to take part in training examinations, working trials, and competitions should traffic-trained. This course is all about the handling of a dog in modern urban traffic. It consists of an obedience element (walking on the lead, walking free, sitting on command, staying combined with the "come!" command) and a practical element which takes place on public roads and squares. The behaviour of the dog towards pedestrians and cyclists coming up from behind is examined, also its behaviour in difficult traffic situations. Then one tests the behaviour of a dog left alone tied on its line for a short time and how it behaves towards other animals. At the end the dog has to pass some obedience exercises in traffic.

Behaviour and obedience

This is a continuation of the traffic-training course, but where the traffic element is dropped and the obedience element expanded. During examinations, the dog is tested for the components such as reacting to a gunshot (noise reaction), jumping over a one-metre hedge and going to, and returning, to a specific place. The dog also has to stay quiet while being physically examined and measured. Before the examination the judge tests the dog for openness. He checks whether the dog can be approached without problems and that it doesn't show any serious behavioural faults.

Endurance

Endurance is important for a Dobermann. After all, it's an active dog that needs plenty of exercise and space. During endurance training, the dog learns to trot (not run or gallop) beside a bicycle. The right gait is important, so that it doesn't over-tire or run its soles sore because of a poor gait. The dog learns to set its pace and spread its strength, so that it can keep up a speed of 8 miles per hour over a long period without tiring.

The examination requires the dog to cover a distance of 13 miles at a speed of between 7.5 and 9 miles per hour (with two pauses). This test proves whether the dog is physically fit and whether heart and lungs function properly.

Guard-dog training

This training consists of three elements: tracking, obedience and guard work (arrest work).
The guard work portion is both interesting and spectacular.
However, the dog must be totally obedient before you can train it.
People often think that arrest training makes a dog spiteful and untrustworthy, but the opposite is true. During guard service a dog must be extremely controlled, disciplined and easy to handle, and for this reason there are high demands in terms of obedience for guard service.

Tracker-dog training

In tracker dog training, the dog must display sure tracking abilities and track a scent that is 1 miles long and at least three hours old. There are seven turns in the scent (matching the terrain). The trace is crossed by two distracting scents a good distance from each other. There are also seven objects at varying distances on the track.

Parasites

All dogs are vulnerable to various sorts of parasite. Parasites are tiny creatures that live at the expense of another animal. They feed on blood, skin and other body substances.

There are two main types. Internal parasites live within their host animal's body (tapeworm and roundworm) and external parasites live on the animals exterior, usually in its coat (fleas and ticks), but also in its ears (ear mite).

Fleas

Fleas feed on a dog's blood. They cause not only itching and skin problems, but can also carry infections such as tapeworm. In large numbers they can cause anaemia and dogs can also become allergic to a flea's saliva, which can cause serious skin conditions. So it's important to treat dog for fleas as effectively as possible, not just on the dog itself but also in its surroundings. For treatment on the animal, there are various medicines: drops for the neck and to put it in its food, flea collars, long-life sprays and flea powders. There are various sprays in pet shops that can be used to eradicate fleas in the dog's immediate surroundings. Choose a spray that kills both adult fleas and their larvae.
If your dog goes in your car, you should spray that too.
Fleas can also affect other pets, so you should treat those too.
When spraying a room, cover any aquarium or fishbowl. If the spray reaches the water, it can be fatal for your fish!

Your vet and pet shop have a wide range of flea treatments and can advise you on the subject.

Ticks

Ticks are small, spider-like parasites. They feed on the blood of the animal or person they've settled on. A tick looks like a tiny, grey-coloured leather bag with eight feet. When it has sucked itself full, it can easily be five to ten times its own size and is darker in colour. Dogs usually fall victim to ticks in bushes, woods or long grass. Ticks cause not only irritation by their blood sucking but can also carry a number of serious diseases. This applies especially to the Mediterranean countries, which can be infested with blood parasites. In our country these diseases are fortunately less common. But Lymes disease, which can also affect humans, has reached our shores. Your vet can prescribe a special treatment if you're planning to take your dog to southern Europe. It is important to fight ticks as effectively as possible. Check your dog regularly, especially when its been running free in woods and bushes. It can also wear an anti-tick collar.

Removing a tick is simple using a tick pincette. Grip the tick with the pincette, as close to the dog's skin as possible and carefully pull it out. You can also grip the tick between your fingers and, using a turning movement, pull it carefully out. You must disinfect the spot where the tick was using iodine to prevent infection. Never soak the tick in alcohol, ether or oil. In a shock reaction the tick may discharge the infected contents of its stomach into the dog's skin.

Worms

Dogs can suffer from various types of worm, The most common are tapeworm and roundworm. Tapeworm causes diarrhoea and poor condition. With a tapeworm infection you can sometimes find small pieces of the worm around the dog's anus or on its bed. In this case, the dog must be wormed. You should also check your dog for fleas, which carry the tapeworm infection.

Roundworm is a condition that reoccurs regularly. Puppies are often infected by their mother's milk. Your vet has medicines to prevent this. Roundworm causes problems (particularly in younger dogs), such as diarrhoea, loss of weight and stagnated growth. In serious cases the pup becomes thin, but with a swollen belly. It may vomit and you can then see the worms in its vomit. They are spaghetti-like tendrils.

A puppy must be treated regularly for worms with a worm treatment. Adult dogs should be treated every six months.

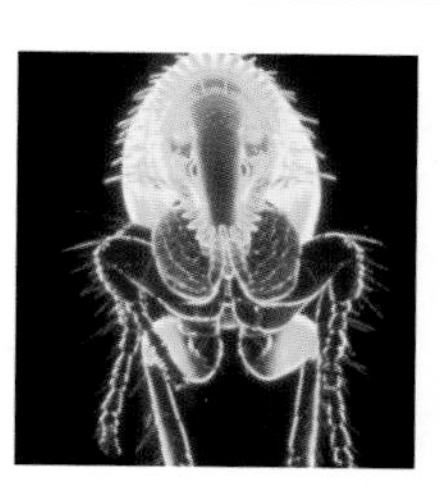

Flea

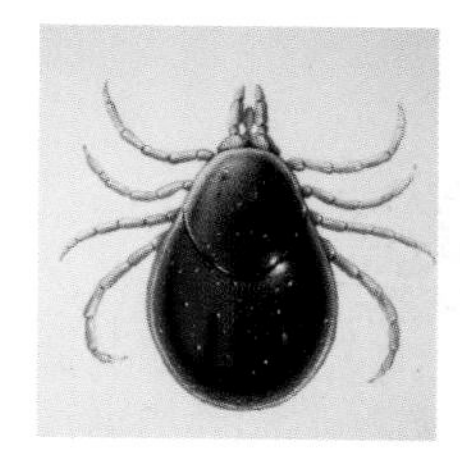

Tick

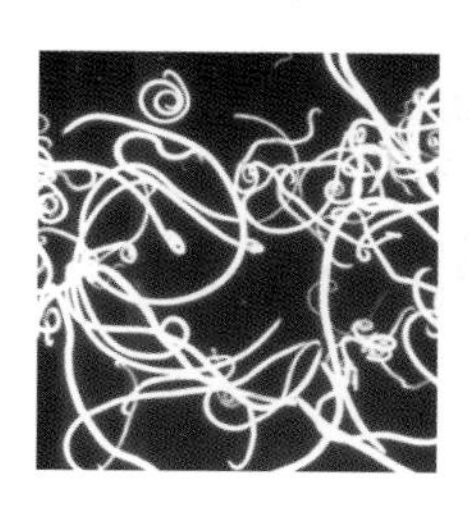

Worm

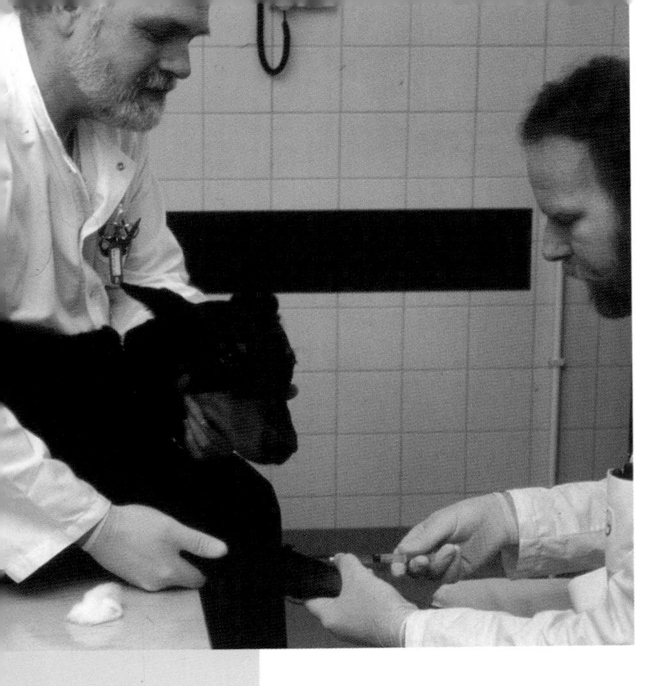

Your Dobermann's health

The space in this small book is too limited to go into the medical ups and downs of the Dobermann. But we do want to give some brief information about ailments and disorders that affect this breed more than other dogs.

Hip Dysplasia (HD)

The first case of hip dysplasia affecting a Dobermann was discovered in recent years. The Dobermann appears particularly vulnerable to it. Fortunately, the number of Dobermanns affected by HD is still low. The breed associations hope that strict monitoring of parent animals will keep it under control. They make examinations for HD mandatory for dogs bred by their members. By means of x-ray checks, dogs are checked for a (slight or serious) form of HD. If they are affected, they may not be used for breeding.

Hip dysplasia is an anomaly in the rear hip joints whereby the hip socket does not properly enclose the head of the thigh bone. This causes infections and bone tumours that are extremely painful. Until recently, it was assumed that HD was primarily caused by genetic factors. Recent investigations, however, indicate that while genetic factors certainly play a role in terms of a dog's susceptibility to HD, external factors such as food quality and exercise appear at least equally important. Limit the chance of HD as far as possible by giving your dog ready-made food of a good brand, and don't add any supplements! Make sure your dog doesn't get too fat. A Dobermann pup should be protected from HD in its first year. Don't let it romp too much with other dogs or chase sticks and balls too wildly. These kinds of games cause the pup to make abrupt and risky movements, which can overburden its soft joints. One important but underestimated factor behind HD is the floor in your home. Parquet and tiled floors are much too slippery for a young dog. Regular slipping can cause complications that promote HD. If you have a smooth floor, it's advisable to lay blankets or old carpet in places the dog uses regularly. Let it spend lots of time in the garden as grass is a perfect surface to run on.

PHTVL/PHPV

This abbreviation stands for Persistent Hyperplastic Tunica Vasculosa Lentis / Persistent Hyper plastic Primary Vitreous. It is a rare congenital eye abnormality. As far as is known, it affects only the Dobermann. It is caused by a disturbance in development whereby remnants of the embryonic blood vessel coat of the lens that feeds the eye with nutrients during pregnancy. The condition is graded from "suspicious", grade 1, to "serious, grade 6.

Entropion and ectropion

These are genetic conditions affecting the eyelids. With entropion the eyelids are curled inwards, with ectropion outwards. Both cause the eyelashes to lay on the eyeball causing irritation, which leads to red, watering eyes.
The eyes become infected and discharge pus. This can cause serious damage to the cornea and eventually even cause blindness. Entropion and ectropion can be corrected surgically.

Tips for the Dobermann

- The Dobermann is a courageous dog full of character, a good up-bringing is essential .
- Buy a Dobermann via the breed association.
- Never let your puppy run endlessly after a ball or stick.
- Don't let your puppy run up and down stairs for the first six months!
- Visit several breeders before you buy a puppy.
- Follow a puppy course with your dog, you'll both benefit.
- Buy your puppy from a reliable breeder.
- Its first car journey is quite an experience for a puppy. Make sure it's a pleasant one.
- Teach your dog good table manners.
- Don't only fight fleas, but their larvae too.
- Never buy a puppy if you couldn't see its mother!
- Hard chunks and plenty to chew on keep the teeth healthy.
- Make sure your dog doesn't get too fat. Not too much to eat and plenty of exercise is the golden rule.
- The Dobermann is an active dog. It will love dog sports!
- A puppy means lots of work and sometimes a few grey hairs.
- Always ask to see the parent dogs' papers. The eyes must have been checked and the elbow and hip joints x-rayed.
- Taking your dog on holiday? Why not?

Other books from About Pets

- The Boxer
- The Cavalier King Charles Spaniel
- The Cocker Spaniel
- The Dalmatian
- The Border Collie
- The German Shepherd
- The Golden Retriever
- The Jack Russell Terrier
- The Labrador Retriever
- The Puppy
- The Rottweiler
- The Budgerigar
- The Canary
- The Cockatiel
- The Parrot
- The Lovebird
- The Cat
- The Kitten
- The Dwarf Hamster
- The Dwarf Rabbit
- The Ferret
- The Gerbil
- The Guinea Pig
- The Hamster
- The Mouse
- The Rabbit
- The Rat
- The Goldfish
- The Tropical Fish
- The Snake

Key features of the series are:

- Most affordable books
- Packed with hands-on information
- Well written by experts
- Easy to understand language
- Full colour original photography
- 70 to 110 photos
- All one needs to know to care well for their pet
- Trusted authors, veterinary consultants, breed and species expert authorities
- Appropriate for first time pet owners
- Interesting detailed information for pet professionals
- Title range includes books for advanced pet owners and breeders
- Includes useful addresses, veterinary data, breed standards.

The Dobermann on the internet

A great deal of information can be found on the internet. A selection of websites with interesting details and links to other sites and pages is listed here. Sometimes pages move to another site or address. You can find more sites by using the available searchmachines.

www.the-kennel-club.org.uk
The Kennel Club's primary objective is to promote in every way, the general improvement of dogs. This site aims to provide you with information you may need to be a responsible pet owner and to help you keep your dog happy, safe and content.

http://www.dobermanns.info
Information on breeders, health, shops, rescue, links to other dobermann pages and much more.

http://www.dobermann.org.uk
A breeders website where you can watch digital video of puppies.

http://www.dpca.org
The Doberman Pinscher Club of America

http://www.geocities.com/Heartland Meadows/7073/#dwapages
Rescues and re-homes dobermanns.

www.k9-care.co.uk
The Self-Help site for dog owners.
A beautiful website with tons of information on dogs. All you need to know about grooming, training, health care, buying a dog, travel and much more.

www.pet-insurance-uk.me.uk
Find low cost pet insurance via this UK pet insurance directory.

www.pethealthcare.co.uk
At pethealthcare.co.uk they believe that a healthy pet is a happy pet. Which is why they've brought together leading experts to create a comprehensive online source of pet care information.

www.onlinepetcare.co.uk
www.onlinepetcare.co.uk was launched in 2001 and contains information about and links to businesses and charities in the midlands area involved in the care and purchasing of domestic animals.

http://champdogs.co.uk
Search the champ dogs database for kennels, stud dogs and litters.

http://dogtraining.co.uk
Your central resource for dog-training, boarding kennels & vets in the UK.

www.k9magazine.com
This refreshing magazine is produced with today's conscientious dog owner in mind and provides a fascinating insight into the latest news, views and gossip from the UK and

world dog scene as well as an easy access point to valuable advice, tips and expert opinion from some of the pet world's leading authorities.

www.rspca.org.uk
The Royal Society for the prevention of cruelty to animals. If you are interested in re-homing a dog (or other animal), pay a visit to your local RSPCA animal center. This site provides information on animal care.

www.mypetstop.com
An international, multilingual website with information on keeping, breeding, behavior, health related issues and much more.

www.waltham.com
Waltham is a firm specialized in pet care and nutrition. On this website you can find more information on pet care, training and diets.

www.aboutpets.info
The website of the publisher of the About Pets book series. An overview of the titles, availability in which languages and where in the world the books are sold.

Breed clubs

Becoming a member of a breed club can be very useful for good advice and interesting activities. Contact the Kennel Club in case addresses or telephonenumbers are changed.

The Kennel Club
1 Clarges Street
London UK, W1J 8AB
Tel: 0870 606 6750
Fax: 020 7518 1058
http://www.the-kennelclub.org.uk/

The Secretary General Scottish Kennel Club
Eskmills Park, Station Road
Musselborough EH21 7PQ
Tel: 0131 665 3920
Fax: 0131 653 6937
www.scottishkennelclub.org
Email:info@scottishkennelclub.org

The Irish kennel club ltd.
Fottrell house, Harold's cross bridge, Dublin 6W. Ireland.
Tel: (01) 4533300 - 4532309 - 4532310.
Fax: (01) 4533237
E-mail: ikenclub@indigo.ie
http://www.ikc.ie/

Doberman Clubs of Great Britain

Birmingham & district Dobermann Club
Sec. Mr P B Rock.
Tel: 01889 566777

Dobermann Club
Sec. Mrs V M Lucas
Tel: 01992 892783

Midland Dobermann Club
Tracey Bostock
3 Whitby Close, Loughborough
Leicestershire, lE11 4FY
Tel: 01509 842852
Fax: 01509 842852
email : secretary@midland-dobermann-club-co.uk
www.midland-dobermann-club.co.uk

North eastern counties Dobermann Society
Sec. Mrs M R Welsh
Tel: 0191 377 0751

North of England Dobermann Club
Sec. Mrs W Meikle
Tel: not available -
For more information
contact the Kennel Club

Northern Ireland Dobermann Club
Sec. Mr D Mcglinchey
Tel: 02894 433778
Scottish Dobermann Club
Sec. Mr S Wright
Tel: 01698 883867

South east of England Dobermann Club
Sec. Mrs M Barton
Tel: 01403 820214
email: mary.barton@tesco.net
http://clik.to/seedc

South West Dobermann Club
Debbie Stansbury
Woodbriar, Hounster Hill
Millbrook, Cornwall
Tel: 01752823106
email : dobes@woodbriar.
freeserve.co.uk
www.southwestdobermann
club.co.uk

Welsh Dobermann Club
Sec. Mrs J E Piper
Tel: 01443 813604

Profile of the Dobermann

Official name:	Dobermann (Pinscher)
FCI-classification:	Group 2: Pinschers and schnauzers, Molossers and Swiss mountain dogs; section 1: Pinchers and schnauzers with training certificate.
Origin:	Germany
Original tasks:	Watch and guard dog
Shoulder height:	Male: 69 - 72 cm (27 – 28 in.) Bitch: 63 - 68 cm (25 – 27 in.)
Weight:	Male: 40 - 45 kg (88 – 100 lbs.) Bitch: 32 - 35 kg (70 – 77 lbs.)
Average life expectancy:	10 - 12 years